Attempts on Death

Attempts on Death

Chawki Abdelamir

Translated by Alan Dent

Smokestack Books
1 Lake Terrace, Grewelthorpe, Ripon HG4 3BU
e-mail: info@smokestack-books.co.uk
www.smokestack-books.co.uk

Poems copyright
Chawki Abdelamir 2020,
all rights reserved.

English translations copyright
Alan Dent, 2020,
all rights reserved.

The text was translated from Arabic to French
by Philippe Delarbre and the author
and published as *Attenter à la mort* in 2016
by Sinbad/Actes Sud (Beirut).

ISBN 9781916312159

Smokestack Books
is represented
by Inpress Ltd

for Baghdad

I

Thirty years later.
On the road from Amman to Bagdad,
14 September 2003

1

Borders... Black with Iraqi women in a wooden cage between Jordanian barbed wire and Iraqi bared wire, corpses in rubber, prey to vultures, birds of the ruins, zenith, trembling star child, H3 Iraqi mouth breathing the air to the depth of the lungs... the road, sure of itself, believing in salvation, but, at each stop, at each turning, I make it hesitate, doubt.

In the distance, windows of lorries, mirrors of the Redskins from westerns, asphalt marked by white lines of melted plastic, huge cardiogram screen of a people being dissected, hills, other hills always blacker, Afghan women's burkas. An invisible lace ties the sky to their neck.

500 kilometres... 412 kilometres... count backwards as far as Bagdad... steps staggering away vertically as far as the gulf of a pyramid of time.

In a lorry, mirthful guards. Their hands, children's hands gripping soft toys, hold Kalashnikovs by the neck. No bird, not even migratory, no tree, not even thorny. Ghost Iraq. Creatures, images trapped in the entrails of emptiness, I distance myself from... I approach...

Two points in me... between them, where am I?
In the distance shines Bagdad... giraffe, a hyena tears its throat.

The car, fly on a dragon's chest, troubles the siesta of an asphalt giant.

Tents... tents... in this homeland of ends, the Bedouin, crouched on the edge of the infinite, camp on the borders of time and place.

Bullets groan in the duration's chest. A generation of deer, at the moment of agony, emits its last rattle. Army, soldiers, mercenaries, dungeons... days of tinned food, life on the spree... On the heights of the Imaginary, I gather the black fruits of the bramble bushes. Dreams and ghosts are silent clothes which cling to my skin, suddenly wind round me in warmth. New exercise: fleeing the claws of exile, skedaddling from the claws of the homeland. Children in ash collars, with sparks in their eyes, asking recurrent questions, elastic playthings...

The living... passing joys and clouds... Iraqi families, dates pressed in palm leaves... In the time of tragedy, the earth's gravity as far as the absorption of bodies....

I remember... Newton – 1959 – Euphrates, the boys' primary school. Between the past's belly and the eviscerated present, Iraq without palm trees is a mother without children.

Oh, palm tree, I know everything about your ancient flowering, your millennial childhood, your invisible kingdom. Beneath your feet bursts a civilisation without deluge or apocalypse, the descendants of kings and tyrants devour themselves. Nothing remains but the traces of dried up oceans, fossils and shells, tides of pain, forests of dry reeds exhaling their music, soul wandering in the night. Here, the abstract, sole master, will remain in the Make-believe of the Iraqis. Sole master to turn its back on the peaks of sense. Sole master to spread over everything the ornamentation of its colours and moons.

On the horizon: delirium and minarets
In the river: orbits and estuaries

I push my way through silhouettes: green, yellow, crowned with Sumerian goddesses, and the halos of imams and saints. Above the fields of palm trees, cries scorch the sky's blue.

The prayer of Anu, the Sumerian father, comes back to me, announcing, while he embraced Inana and offered her a cup of plant blood, the spurting of the Euphrates from between her legs.

I seize caliph Al-Mansour's hand, tracing with his compass the arc of the defensive walls and the palace's barracks, forgetting the portals of an Abbassid night spread wide above thousands of nights, of dawns of jinns.

I spy out, in the middle of a territory as arid as a cake of warm bread, a song of yellow reeds. I extinguish, with the flesh of my palms, the fire which burns Tawhidi's books, the crowns of flames which consume Hallaj's forehead and Abdullah ibn Muqaffa's arms.

I bury myself, in Baghdad, in the cellars of a tavern. I see Hassan ibn Hani getting ready to extract a soul from the entrails of an old vat of wine.

I question Mutanabbi:
Where is the land of Iraq?
He replies:
From Tourban, where we are...
There, the offering.

2

The stupor, in the eyes of the living
is situated in the vigil kept
by an extinct species of birds
which took the route to exile
and came back, never

And death, they say
is on the look-out
for an antiquated organ
which plays without pause

The Sumerian lyre and the lady of Warka
with the return of the schoolchildren
and the piping of little souls
torn like lilies
which rediscover their shelter

The tears
flow between the faults
formed by the questions
which fall like meteors

Unearthed by a southern peasant
in a royal cemetery in Ur
extorted by a western tourist
a divine little statue
is fear

In each body
pain
is a mausoleum

The Euphrates
which sprang from Anu's phallus
flows into the pubic triangle
of the Arabian peninsula

3

Descent of the children
into the sky's liver
Descent of the ivy
onto the heights of glances
Descent of the palm tree
into the raucousness of a flute
Descent of the papyrus
along our passions
Descent of the birds
into our chests' cages
Descents of the assassin
into the lap of heavens
Descent of heaven
into the muezzin's throat
Descent of Allah
into the throat cutters' litany
Descent of death
as far as Allah
Descent of the survivors
as far as death
Descent of the village
beyond its viaticum
Descent of the area
into an informer's notebook
Descent of the sleepless night
into the dawn of the disappeared
Descent of the river
in a shooting ship
Descent from the balcony
in a shout from the horizon
Descent of the ruins
Descent... descent

4

Allah Hussein is Iraqi. He lives in Baghdad, on bits of gold extracted from weapons and electronic devices thrown onto tips in the open air.

>Gold from the cemeteries
>Gold from queens' necklaces
>Gold from taps
>Gold from minarets
>Gold from crowns
>Gold from teeth
>Gold from the innards of weapons
>Gold from the innards of mausoleums
>Gold from scalpels
>Gold from fingers
>Gold of life
>Gold of death
>Iraqi gold
>Gold

Baghdad, November 2003

II

1

Smoke gathering
in the skin of duration

Shadows, whale
engulfing other shadows
Days, bursts of chaos
splitting the eye of place

Vine women
bunch children
crumbling from their chests

Ends taking their revenge
on the origin's star

Baghdad
An empire inaugurates
a radiant golden age

But a strange light
a strange light
rises from the young and blighted tombs
and from coal
from faces and shouts
dazzling tears
from a kingdom here below
dripping onto the sky

Are they souls' footsteps
butterflies on lamps, fluttering in eternity
Souls which shine
which shine for ever

2

Inima Ilich

When from Al-Sawwad
the vapour of the dead
like water vapour
rises towards the sky
And from water we created
all living things

This night of 20 March 2003
according to the terrestrial calendar

The souls of Iraqis
tumble in the corridors of the beyond
trouble the sleep of Sumer's gods
The divinities
take off their cloaks
come down to earth
discover the hovels of the Euphrates' peasants
the beds of gnawed reeds
the tunnels of torture
the tanks of nitric acid
and spend their rotten night
among the fish drying on the roofs

3

The bullets which pierce
the third millennium's wall
and reach Baghdad
penetrate the stained glass
eyes of the divinities
which divide in the temples
pagan from monotheistic gods
life and death
They rebuild the timber of sense
and turn Al-Sawwad's head
towards the Supreme Pain

In Babylon
the geranium's blood
uranium's blood
dry
beneath the gardens of the suspended bodies

Thick clouds
where the dead hollow out shelters
for children who scatter
in Baghdad's streets
Wings
for the last time
touch the earth

4

Yesterday, the river awoke
it saw
Iraq as the cross of the cardinal points
There was a god
ignoring legends and History's layers
a god without flood
without an ark
without verses
without psalms
a god who drags Mesopotamia's sons
in convicts' irons
as far as the global sanctuary
and installs there his temple and the day of Judgement

5

It isn't day
this match
useless except for burning
seasons, rivers, dried out clouds
in the land of Iraq

It isn't day
this combustion of chaos
dust of nothingness
on the houses, the faces
and the calcified palm-groves
in the land of Iraq

It isn't day
this ray passing
between the rubbish and the eyes of the passers-by
guided by satellites
on the wing of the Tomahawk
as far as the children's playground
in the forsaken night
in the land of Iraq

It isn't day
this obscure spectre
driver of Jupiter's chariot
come from this side of the shadow ocean
to steal the sunrise
in the land of Iraq

It isn't day
this cemetery lamp
which illuminates the time
not the place
in the land of Iraq

6

Man

    man who isn't a person
    man not knowing who he is
    man not knowing who they are
    man trampled by corpses
    man tree
    man in rags
    man an empty flour sack
    man barring the way
        to the clouds, to the seasons, to armies
    man burnt alive whose body remains
    man assassinated having lost his corpse
    man asleep, his dream on the screens
    man facing the tanks entering Basra
    man standing

    Iraq

7

Jassem Alwan
in Nassyria
is burying his little girl
He ties the swaddling clothes of the little corpse
to the throat of the sky
whose cry dissipates from the top of the minaret

Jassem Alwan
on a hill in Ur
has placed his little girl in a grave
He wonders over the mystery of the improvisation
of a small step
between eternal and origin
a step going backwards

He scrutinises the ends which stick to their canes
and will never again die
He examines a Sumerian tablet
and takes the pulse of the Creature

The scene, its visible and invisible contours,
is enclosed in a British soldier's visor
who disturbs with his battle dress and rifle
the first epics' dust
and the last battles' *toz*

Jassem Alwan
came back from his hill
half dead
half a killer

Looking for the grass
stolen by the snake
he left
to conquer life

8

The twentieth of a month
on the threshold of the third millennium
of the birth of the crucified
whose blood is the ink of historians
Baghdad awoke

At the spot chosen by caliph Al-Mansour
on the Tigris' haunches
become the planet's lung
Baghdad awoke

In an azure-stone incrusted bed
and guarded by spirits
facing the whinnying
from the frozen deserts of Mongolia
Baghdad awoke

From its bedroom where the gardens, the walls
survey the Tigris
to shrug its shoulders
abandon its bed
wander in the alleys, the patios and the Turkish baths
Baghdad awoke

Opening its bundle
deploying its soothsayers' evil rolls
sitting planet earth on its lap
singing its godesses' lullabies
and its madness's psalms
She, who has never slept again
Baghdad

9

The Simoon
fills time's crevasses
the ends' fissures
where
dust with its back to the light
the debris of corpses
crumbs of destinies
dance
All-coloured rainbow
between the non-sky
and the non-earth
Air which Iraq breathes out

10

A new-born clings to the breast
the breast to a woman
the woman to a corpse
the corpse to a wall
the wall to a projectile
the projectile to a cloud
the cloud to a sky
the sky to the Milky Way
the Milky Way to the universe
the universe to Allah
Allah, Him, at the heart

11

Reporters
The scene is in full swing
the cameras stuff themselves with the dead and ruins
the loud-speakers with cries and explosions
dust, human flesh
scene transmitted by the satellites and the moons of Baghdad
as far as the mouths of the empire

Reporters
who extract minutes of blood
from agonising bodies
and drag them flesh trembling
to operating tables

I.r.a.q.i. f.r.a.g.m.e.n.t.s

Live fish
Thrown, punctually, quivering on the slab
The metropolises expect their fresh blood

Reporters

12

The woman
shouts at the pit
the pit
shouts at the woman

Face to face
body to body
entrails against entrails

The woman
the pit
two females
defying one another, square up

The woman trembles
shakes the pit's haunches
the pit leaps
swallows its saliva

Two women
arguing
over a man's
remains

III

1

Pink planet
staggering in the Baghdad night
on the heights
in the lower depths,
silhouettes and corpses pass one another
breathing the original air

Language
anguish's frozen child
feels the homeland
body and time
take refuge within it

The wave the Tigris rejects
melts in me
bridges and moments stretch out
without reaching the bank

2

In the dried-out marshes
the reed stems
have the majesty
of granite columns

The living
are puddles
a corpse floats
Thales's cloth on the secular ocean

In the marshes at night
between the two dead fish
and the orbits of distant stars
between frontiers
of here-below and the beyond
souls oscillate

3

Apocalypse is woman
exited from life
in spite of temptations
chants and southern epics
in the very place where I was born

I'm not the bird from the flood
having reached dry land
I'll have gone back to the point of departure

For me, my nail
For eternity, its clay

The stele is not my limit
it's a hand
only I know how to use
the other hand

O brothers
chained to my cursed paradises
here is my sacred ember
I came into the world to pour out my gifts
prophets and depots implore peoples and destinies
since the present is crumbs
between the arms of my rivers

O present, take me out of memory
I know you, boulder
Against you I scrape my body
rag which falls to pieces

The dark of me
Mirror

Wait for me, shadow
I am the creative night of your perishability
The bar of Alif in me is a mast not a bayonet
I am not a boat shrouded in fog
berthing on the distant sky

The mount of absence
today taller than thirty years
hasn't kept me from the flood

Wait for me, love
I'll return
at the very moment when I'll unfurl
this hell's apocalypse

4

What is this cloud of the sky
which calls itself the sky of clouds

What is
this me

5

O palm tree
have you betrayed the beyond
to be cursed on an earth between two rivers
and remain mother
pregnant with a foetus
which, in you, is born and dies

Here are its signs and its days
Here are its mirrors and its moons
They break against the wave of the southern sea
which has left its bed
Peoples and kingdoms vanish
beneath the disappeared blue
Poets and seers from between two rivers
wandering in skies and languages
sing its waiting

Tonight
I will climb a ziggurat
whose ruins I'm a unique trace of
I beg that from the breasts of the flood
might spring forth solid earth
Eve from Adam's chest

I see the river
depositing the black spume of its orbits
I see the hanging bunches
wet nurse's breasts

I see the dead imploring the seasons
to give birth to a fifth
I see on my father's tomb
a ruby
take its blood

6

Take this day by the neck
drag it towards the abyss
or the depths of a pit
interrogate it
What did this new-born do
to be put to death
he who never learnt to spell my name

Repeat, repeat the question
until he replies
So open up my embers
and bathe in my springs

Never have I sublimated a promise
which is The Promise
a truth which is The Truth
a land which is Iraq

7

To you
Burnt wick at the heart of cold night
Baked earth, slab
Destiny's obelisk
Bunch of grapes, wine before being harvested
Cup of plenitude and poetry
To you
land of Iraq
birth tomb
hello

Baghdad, 9 April 2004

IV

1

Here is the land of the last clouds
those which, shower after shower
plunge me between abyss and abyss
Earth bartering its ruins and its fields
against the steps which don't return

Here is a prophetic earth
Earth absent yesterday on my return
interrogating its sand and its sky
It left in its bed
before leaving everything
an inanimate homeland

Here is an earth
ever pregnant
for it, we have eviscerated bellies
scorched skies
without ever making shoot forth the cry of new-born

Here is a proscribed earth
an earth in me beyond reach
an earth in me putting itself to bed

2

O Tigris
from the top of a wall full of bullet holes
I surprise Baghdad
Young girl, she knots her legs around your neck
and plays on your shoulders

O father
you flow between the caliph's bed
and the rising of creation
What seal has engraved on your side
a Bedouin slave
I knew
your night
deeper than the ossuary
I always hear at the hour of your dawn
the cries of dead cocks

Tell me, father
where will you assemble your prodigious children
Beneath the tent of the day gone by
raised on my spine
beneath the roof of a day
which rubs its eyes
coming out of a long sleep
in the cellars of torture and the parched pits

O father, O Tigris
make of me a wave
which severs me from myself
or a river bank
which never, promise it
you will never try to violate

3

Hurlers of little arrows
never will you pierce my wound
The arrows which reach me
are unleashed from a string
tying my ribs to a rainbow

Stabbing my childhood
hurlers of little arrows
you have only grown older
You are nothing but a curse
idols I have renounced
statues I've destroyed

But at the end of every joust
your arrows
gather
black spume of my torments

One day I will set alight
the secrets of my night
and will leave
meteor after meteor
my body to crash down
in my confines

4

Euphrates
Blind one which saw
arm of flood, pond of the Creation
Help me, close my eyes
So they may see with yours

Euphrates
Tide which washes the orbit of sunsets
and the forehead of suns
Take my hand
Lead me to the southern spectres
Show me how the convicts
of wars and tragedies
colour your waves with red clay

5

Baghdad
return
bird which struggles in me
which I can't catch

Sunset which rises
in my wanderings

Return
which even returned
I daren't confront

The departure
covers me
like lichen
the sea's rocks

6

I catch my days by the knees
woman howling
at the moment of giving birth

Blind
I grope
my cane the river's border
I arrive at myself

Darkness
scrutinizing with its seers' eyes
and which, from a fistful of millennial roots
attracts clouds to itself

From the belly of a dead whale
loomed the prophetic present
towards the palm trees its flood's boats
the survivors rush

Baghdad, April 2004

V

1

In Baghdad's National Library
I read, blind seer
between lines of cinders
I touch the text's carbon
like a child lightly stroking its father's head
as death approaches

A chair from an office
skeleton with blackened limbs
gripping a still white
leaf

From the window
smashed open by the flames' arms
a dishevelled palm tree rises
and recites canticles out loud
It sorts the index of lost titles
and the major chapters of the fire's history
in Baghdad's parchment

I left
In my hand, my pen
a match

2

Of the massacre
all that remains are shoes
a pile of tanned skins

Shoes
which enter neither mosques
nor the ancestors' living-rooms
and stay, as is customary, on the threshold

Death prefers
naked feet and bodies
the worst fabric
resists it more than skin and bone

Shoes of all shapes
of all kinds, all out of fashion
for children who
generation after generation
have inherited them
without tongues
without laces

Shoes
Nothing remains of their owners
which justifies a burial
apart from reddish stains
shades of spume
not polishing
and which can be covered with earth
in the simulacrum of an interment

Shoes
from a distance little pyramids
recalling those built by Hulago Khan
in this very place, seven centuries earlier
same geometry
same place
same materials

In Baghdad
the only difference
between pyramids of shoes today
and pyramids of heads yesterday
is a link
to the spirit of the time

3

In Abbasid Baghdad
a poisoned corpse
wrapped in a carpet
thrown on a bridge
One thousand two hundred and forty-three years after
one thousand three hundred corpses
drowned, poisoned, crushed
thrown on the same bridge
a bridge in Baghdad

Baghdad
the spherical, the abbasid
rotates on herself
masters her trajectory
in her, since Al-Mansour
windmills
millions of pilgrims

This Wednesday 13 August 2005
the Tigris had three banks
The third was a place of pilgrimage

Iraqis
for millennia
dried out dates
falling from their bunches
onto an earth
paradise between two rivers

Sailors
of the first seas
thrown up by the sea
burying masts and the bones of boats
in cemeteries
called epic
coming back to cultivate the earth, rivers
marshes of reeds and of children
imploring their new mausoleum
the Departure

The anticipated Imam
his dome
haloed with processions of walkers
of banners and stars
The victorious hero
raised on shoulders
advances in a coffin

Iraqis
indifferent to the springs
swimming against the current
preferring estuaries in death

They walk
domes and palm trees
fraternising with storms
and decorating themselves with simoon

The path arrives
they don't

In the cracked sky
unshod
they nourish once more the walk
where fire and light melt
days and chaos
faces and clay

Iraqis
crossing the river
towards the sanctuary of the imam
unaware
that the river
is the imam
who, towards Allah
will guide their steps on the water

Paris, October 2005

VI

I break the rib of the present
to accomplish my night

Between 'flanks and fronts'
the first uterus awoke
carrying within a moon
which polishes its mirrors and lights up
It comes in so I can leave
and the past will meet me

O night, O din
Is the divine the clock which breaks
when the vision is realised

I have a body not a present
so I go
I place a foot without the other
I break like an antique vase
I pluck the hours
like a wave the grains of sand

I unearth a face
among those which, in procession, in an instant
set off for the beyond
I wake my skeleton
that sleep
has putrified
on the martyr's pillow

I hold out my full cup
to the hand of a loved one
ready to drink me from my eye-sockets

So I go
I strangle my clouds with ink
I drag my sky by its horns
on the tattooed tombs of feathered steles

Feathers, eyebrows for the eyes of the abyss
matter before matter
signs to measure
the trembling of hell's lands

In the night of spectres
no element inherits from me
no origin celebrates me
Inflammable naphtha
kerosene for flight over the beyond
teach me to fear my blood
teach me to penetrate this world
solely with your open arms

The grey shell
is day sleeping in a pearl
How many days will I break
to put together a collar
around your neck

Talk to me of rags not idols
of springs not towers
of years and men sated in you
like offering of Arab goddesses
chomping on the grass of rest
and the pulse of clay
Everything a kiss
alone turned red

I have neither
lips
nor clay nor ink

I break the rib of the present
To accomplish my night

Here is my talisman
Gathered on the paths of genesis
Between the god's canines

The Arab peninsula
celebrated by suns and tribes
drags its skeleton
to the continents' portals

Manpower in migration
waiting for banners
come from the past
returned to the past

among hostaged people
in the present's purgatory

>   Dream
>   A bird with its throat cut
>   its blood formed on my shirt
>   Suddenly a child from the south
>   come from forests of reeds in the fens
>   shouted my name
>   the bird flew towards an unknown land
>   the child ran after him
>   and buried itself in the mist

O child, come to me
We will break the globe's jar
illuminated by these millions of stars
in the sky of your eyes

Come, child
and you, the present
rotted like a cloth from the start of time
go back to hell
From you, I have only
the sigh of a little coffin
leant against the back of thousands of Mesopotamian years
Birth knows nothing of the path of beginning
The shrouds are too short
to be the crime's curtain

In the night of spectres
of you, I have only
these extinguished years

I cross the water of my rivers
passing through the flood of my rivers
to get to the bank of my rivers

My night
That night
is inscribed stone
name after name
on the cardinal points

Towards the south
the south of the south
on its knees crawls
a strange sun
My night
is black stone
coagulated pilgrimage
turning around itself

O Sumerian refuge
carpet of dreams woven from my generation's horror
ceiling of rusted stars
days in tatters
orgasm of spectres

O night
my rudder

For Iraqi terraces
draping themselves in the Milky Way
for women laying out
on the night's balconies
feathers and carded cotton
For a deliverance nudity
for a trembling hand
on meeting another hand
for a star progressing through me
I walk
sleepwalker in his death

On the southern paths
the shepherd Euphrates
guide
towards the homeland of estuaries
troops of gods, of lovers and of peasants.

VII

1

We will disembowel the dragon
you would say
on the threshold
of our clay house

The earth around us
changes into an era of fire
and reconciles the wound and the knife
are we the mother
who, in the tomb of the divine
devoured its ancestry

We have neither shadow
nor sun
beyond what comes to us from the belly of the beyond
nor food
beyond which what grows in our palms
Our brothers quench their thirst
at black, red, green and white springs
backs of the first pedigree
raise steles and complaints
for our martyrs
and raise, on their shoulders, the dragon
dragons
with mouths striated with traces
of the cemeteries of our loved ones
submerged by the living

Dragon
at whose feet they display
necklaces of their past
jewels of their first wisdom
at whose feet they kneel
the captives of Hattin

Now
now, you would say
we will bleed the earth
we will extract the roots of verses
we will reunite
in the origin's turning

2

Alone, in Baghdad
I lightly touch on the riverbank
a branch, an earth
I see all things come running
snake draped in my innards
I attract them into my lap
I climb the terrace of a night holed with stars
I stretch out, shadow in the sunset
and I sleep, knocked over by the constellations

The mysterious signs blink around me
summer insects
bullets, the rumbling of the helicopter
chop up the horizon on my bed
drag me from sleep
flood me with a phosphorescent light
guiding towards my body the ghosts
they come to sleep there for

Alone, in Baghdad
I unearth the roots of the garden
looking for a body
body disappeared from a morgue
or in the hospital's garage
of a father muffled
in a woollen multi-coloured cover
Body carried in a village coffin
on the top of a Chevrolet
heading towards a desert's cemetery
where the dead are dying of thirst
and the living of madness

where the near ones are bits of embers
sleeping in limbo
waiting for the return of their loved ones

Alone, in Baghdad
blind shepherd
whose flock is an eastern wind
I run behind a hoard of echoes
I read in the hand of the marsh
and in the neck of the palm tree

There I see a breast
from which nothing forms but dry blood
a day chased from History
paths which retrace their steps
a body without a head walking
in the streets of Baghdad

I see the curds of black days
brandish the banners of Taff
crawling on their knees
drawn by the song of the camel driver
haranguing the step
on the melted tar of the Straight and Narrow
to arrive at Ali's tomb
and to visit it
corpses in procession

Alone, in Baghdad
I cast off an earth
baked by the suns of my first years
tattooed with embers and henna
I walk with the river entreaty
pouring out vertically
I finger the gaudy stones of the rosary
pages of tragedies
on an earth between two days
between two rivers

Alone, in Baghdad
on the map kept
by the arch and the sacred
I glimpse riots of stray dogs
burying their noses
in puddles of names

Alone
and everything abandons me

3

From a Baghdad window
the river, tonight, showed me its silhouette
So I rushed down a path
cut out only by the current

I threw away the clay masks
I saw the reeds fraternising
the pam trees panic
I heard the bleating of stones

I said to myself
I will penetrate the depths of an earth
which doesn't know me
there I will see a tormented season
and toothless years

Higher than the wing of death
in a seagull's shudder
I will follow the blind flight of clouds of birds
which, with their beaks
peck the clouds' breast
and snatch the goldfish
shimmering by the river's edge

I cross destinies and flood
those who have hidden exoduses
which bury the Mede tribes
carried away by Utnapishtim's ark
to a land of chests of tubercular reeds
and bones of sand filled ports
Land
floating palm tree trunks

I enter
the reed calvary
which coughs night and day

There I see
seated on a bed of palm tree fibres
a child of ten
whose chest is a tablet engraved with prayers
whose eyes shine
wet field
of the time before dawn
He asked me to read him
the verses inscribed on his chest
I couldn't hear my voice
I saw in his pupils
Koranic chapters of crystal break
The night was
hyena black
lying on a bed of flames

Behind the struggles of soaked reeds
like loaves of bread on the water
the boats in the marsh from Sumer
the fantasy fish
skewered by a harpoon
a floating tomb
and the bellowing of the hydra
protecting the divine belt
padlocking Ishtar's sex

A little body
Doumouzian ship
adrift on the southern coasts
and that peasants
setting off for towns and ports
towed to the city
with a thousand barracks and walls

Baghdad

Paris, 2005

VIII

1

Beneath a breast sky
I climb on the rock of my descent
The nation is a water-skin
which, drop by drop, empties
There is no other home
but my palms

After one thousand five hundred years of digging
in and on the brows
I throw days
pebbles they ricochet
on an asphalt's mirage

Picnic tablecloths
McDonald's bags
Skeletons of springs
Arabs placing their feet in the era

My poem is a white night
moon hill
with a parched look
torrent which won't prostrate itself
to the estuary

Arab obedience
Thanks

Tourists unearthing
villages and tombs
we unearth your entrails
looking for fossils of Arab letters

Our poems are *muallaqat*
our gorges, black stones
The geography is crypt
of your monotheistic temple
Arab obedience
thanks

2

Clouds of human blackness
announced by the Baghdad sky
this 13 July 2005
in the latest weather forecast

The verb in the present
is a booby-trapped jar
watch out for conjugation

In the alleys of Karradah
a white sail
and a soul's desire
to wallow there

Cries
wind against shields

Blood soaked air
help me to hear
what your breezes full of lives and larva
reveal this July night

Believing
your prayers
are booby-trapped skin
which you project
towards Allah

Your faith
is a child's nails
clenched on dawn's
shirt
Being is a bowl
of life's concentrated acid

A road's signpost
diverts my route towards the sky
mixing there
passers-by's shoes
with the wings of angels

weapons are fruit peelings
thrown to tribes hardly extracted from
the original famines

Who said: Iraq has two rivers
I confirm it: we saw nothing

Clouds of dead Iraqis
climb
the minarets of Arab towns
and call
to a new dawn

O beloved earth
will your sand stop
filling our eyes

our dreams
our notebooks

The thick breezes
are intoxicating on this cold night
of expectancy
between them and us
there are blood links

The day on each street corner
transforms into a gigantic stained-glass window
surrounding with a halo the sacrificial altar

3

My mother reads from a book every day
the same book
She scrutinizes it, murmurs it
spells it out, declines it every moment
She reads it, re-reads it
listens to her listening
My mother remembers, forgets, remembers
each reading of the same book is, for her, dedicated to a someone dead
My mother has read only this book
Nothing else. Not even a letter
Her reading is a symphony
that she alone executes with all the instruments
And death alone accompanies her

My mother, after each reading
indicates another dead person for a companion
The next day she goes to the cemetery
taking with her all the reading garnered during the season
Before each grave
she flicks through with her eyes
the pages which enclose her heart
and those which enclose the grave
Death takes her reading
leaving between her hands only
the book

My mother neither likes nor hates reading
she is neither illiterate nor literary
she opens a door and enters
there where there is neither front or back
neither exterior nor interior
except the voice
her voice which inundates the arches
of presence
and absence

4

Burn the notebooks
Here's another grammar lesson

Draw Being into an allegory
Cut him up like a lamb
Let the cardinal points
change places
Let pronouns
become indefinable

Let coordinating conjunctions
cut necks
dismember bodies
Let rules and laws
pull themselves up
elegantly and cleanly
like weeds

The Arab language
sends the sun back
to its original chaos
Arabness today
is tragedy which holds forth
millennial cloud
which, in an antique amphora
pours out still its rain

Speeches are only frogs
croaking in ponds
worms devour verbs
before conjugation
senses are women
for Arab virility

IX

1

Dhad Island

Dhad
of verses
home of princely hostages
guard of an amazed crowd
and Eden's columns

Dhad
of antique banners
of towers which lick the clouds' salt
and suck the moons' milk
She lays out her thighs
She taxes the rain
Zakat and tithe for her caliphate

Dhad
of barracks
She digs
jails
for palm trees and willows
and in mothers' bellies
shelters for guards

She knows what millions of leaves tell
each autumn in the forest
She strips before time
the snake of his skin
She makes
of the moon lovers
in the Gypsies' valley
a castle for her old troopers
those who, lost for long years in the desert
returned astride hills

Dhad
the immolated
She who leads the flocks into the fields
guides the passers-by
makes the stained-glass silhouettes sparkling and enormous
of cement towns
leads workers to workshops
gets drunk in pubs
accompanies to their end
the limousine, the blind one
the condemned
comforts prisoners and the sick

Dhad
dragged by death's phantom
left
with her descendants
her domes
her ears of grain and nights of famine
her lightning
her passion, her fear, her poor
her past, her remains
women, coffee, bread
the black stone
stones of all colours
the river and its rising
the djinns of maleficent dawns

The shrouds covering her sex
she gleans talismans, necklaces and poems
haunts the dreams
roams behind mysteries
with angel's wings
and mummy's eyes

To flee
to flee forever
the traces of the immolated

The immolated is dead
Is she dead the immolated

2

'In their nests
are birds
whose hearts
are soaked and dry
redcurrants and moist dates'
Imrû'al-Qays

Stop, you the two
Imrû'al-Qays
whose word was sovereign
you, the singular duo
who, come from the vault's vestiges
fraternise only with the distant
and desert only the ruins
towards you come hills and stags
between your legs soak the silken women
and the temple virgins

You are the two
who die one after the other
the steppes chant your rhymes
neither the eagle nor the vulture
pecks your face
or troubles your opulence

Stop, you the two
Imrû'al-Qays
whose word was sovereign
you and the destiny which caught up with you
and the voice which led you
you and your camel
you and exile
cry, drink deep of blows
before getting the tent ready
and declaiming your poems

O Imrû'al-Qays
haven't you been in your intoxication
a refuge
in whose heart you made
day and night
your pillows
and slipped them beneath the body of the loved one
the sands and your voice caught fire
from embers and passion
you entwined it like the pleura
you suspended yourself from its eyelashes
Imrû' al-Qays
whose word was sovereign
I am the mount turbaned by clouds
hung with a Yemeni necklace
behind me, in an anguished drunkenness
villages, ruins and the peninsula's virgins hurled themselves

Stop, you the two
Imrû' al-Qays
whose word was sovereign
Blood which falls drop by drop
from vengence's cloud
on the mountain chain
on the hawthorn buds
on the peninsula's Wadis
separated between its past and the past
and from where came days
she-camel covered in tar
Stop, you the two
Imrû al-Qays
whose word was sovereign
You are the cup filled with songs from the epics
You are, at the crossroads of the soul and the body
the feast's carpet
for horses, women and vigils
You are the sky
stars knotted to the rocks of the mounts
You are the ravine at sunset
palms shining after rain

You who sacrificed your she-camel
to lovers not to the gods
to virgins not to temples
On their feet not on the sacred threshold
you spread the musk
For them you ignited
rhyme's dry wicks

Behind their shadows, you ploughed the desert
And for them, you stripped the dawn
Stop, you the two
Imrû'al-Qays
whose word was sovereign
hung between gods and rites
for your desire's fur
and your body's blade
in the abrahamite and divine Kaaba
asleep in the birds' hearts
redcurrants and moist dates
you put on your shirt tattooed with wounds
so that breath after breath
priest's lamp
hung above the abyss
extinguishes your soul

Stop, you the two
Imrû al-Qays
whose word was sovereign
You who runs across the regions
behind the drop which quenches
the sands' anger
or the viaticum of a proscribed soldier
Newborn you carried
the kingdom in your arms
In Hadramaout, in Dammoun
I was looking for a necklace belonging to Afra, your beloved
or a spear from the invasion of Andel, your longed-for village
And you were there, you the two
Imrû al-Qays
whose word was sovereign
as if you'd never sat up for a night in Dammoun
as if you'd never seen a raid on Andel

And off you went

X

Letter Received by My Father after His Death

Father,
In Beirut I found my way back to the palm tree, that palm tree in the fields to whose foot, remember, you led me, palm tree holding its rejection by the hand, before exile wrenched me from the land of your hands.

I see it today, I touch it, I tremble and it shudders. The tree which covered me in its dew when as a child I climbed it and devoured its dates.

Father, I've found my way back to the palm tree. It is shrouded in iodine, foam and shells and I'm in front of it, pagan poem hanging in exile's Kaaba, while there is no other adored idol here but my corpse awaited like the Mahdi.

Father,
When my words get to you, your body will be nothing but one more word in the dictionary of this Iraqi nothingness recluse in the great cemetery of the Nadjaf desert.

When my words get to you, you will read them, letter after letter, and you will find yourself with the smile of a child gathering the first fruits from the tree planted and tended by its own hands. Your eyes, my eyes, will shine with the same tear that I feel forming between my lashes at the moment I discover you haven't entirely disappeared.

From you I inherited my pupil, its colour, its shape, the way my eye blinks. I feel a part of you lives still in my sockets. Thus together let's watch, henceforth, the river of Iraqi blood, embers and gold.

Father,

Do you remember the fields of Moyechieh to the south of the el-Chiok Souk, there, where in Hour, rises the head of the Euphrates and its bloody flank? You introduced me to an old palm tree which took my hand and held me close under the eyes of Soubat, that hundred-year-old peasant, whose age neither he nor you knew and which saved me from the Euphrates' decline.

You knew that between men and palm trees, there is an invisible, ineffable body, that on the day of its breaking there would be rupture.

That rupture, I see its image everywhere in the streets of Beirut. Beirut where the palm trees themselves take the road to exile, while the Euphrates has dried up in its bed.

Father,

Look at this palm tree. Isn't it the one in whose arms you died? Compresses of hemp soaked in spindrift surround its neck. It faces the Mediterranean winds. It has the detachment of the person who has drunk the milk of Creation's spring, the endurance of the person who draws their stature from vital blood and the disturbance of the person returned from Purgatory. I know all the reasons for its difficulties, for the austerity of its appearance, of its hesitation in recognizing its friends. It can't put up with the height of the cliffs here, nor that of the eyes or the houses.

Can it, facing the sea, plunge its vision into the infinite while the blue is, for it, only celestial.

It has known only the river it inherited from the south, its father, and through legend, its mother. From the day when time mixed with the flood, it lived, with its river, the play of the spate and the low tide. The spate which, never, managed to reach its full height, which, without respite returned to its bed, carrying, in its flow, all the hamlets, prey camped on its banks.

Here, in Beirut, the highest tide, with its spray and its roar, doesn't have waves high enough to merely wet its heels.

Remember father, when, in its celestial bed, Doumouzi,
harassed by the summer wind, fertilised it.
The clay as a mirror for its plaits, the tides were lakes where it washed its feet. It called to itself drums and songs from the south to cry for its dead.
It knew how to bring the rivers back to the estuary,
The loam to the fields,
The disappeared to the village,
Drowned children to their mothers

    O father
    O palm tree
    My obelisk.

for Beirut

Paradise

Your hands at their highest
paradises suspended
I am not
Adam

Absence

Time I didn't live
Town I knew
without having known it
I have no other steps but those of the hypothesis
Seagull
with wings which melt into the mists of an atlas
wings also of a bird
crushed on the asphalt

I will not come back
from a two-winged flight
I have chosen
Absence

Pearl

My wife is my shell
which of us is the pearl

I have for you the gaze
of a blind sailor for the sea
Don't speak to me of embrace
nor of return to earth

O straw bird
your stone branch
has flowered

The carcass of an exploded car
in the road
redraws
the black storm clouds

In Beirut, hammers
are ready to redress
the sea's waves

The stricken bird
clasps beneath its wings
a sky

The tattoo
is a fish
in your back's lake

Are you
necklace of clouds
which rain
on my day's thirst

The electromagnetic sentence
thousands of kilometres away
connects my lips
to your limbs' flames

Nostalgia's root
Does not heal
From desire's rain

A blue boat
Parts the sea into two abysses
Your eyes
Lay your hand
on the white necklace of the night
Dazzle of a fire
which would grill us
like chestnuts

I learn to be born
in a sentence
to bury myself
in its carnivorous carollas

Road
here as far as the eye can see
No, I will not come back
No, I will not leave

You, me
We are the place
Which drinks the milk
Of the cardinal points

Entrust your desert to my palm
following the example of a key
in the hands of a child
Close it again
Go to sleep
in my arms

The Messenger's Cloud

I do not cross
I harbour
A desert

I go back to Beirut
The arrow returns to the archer
The messenger is cloud

My lighthouse
 will never admit
which of us is the river bank
what are the poet's secret words

The woman
who doesn't attract the mast
is ocean
hung on drawing pins

The sea got out of breath
the fishermen twisted
the waves' linen

Never has your body's flute
been quiet for a moment

Unblemished
by the foam
and a wave beneath the sheets

I know
the look your left shoulder has
when I suddenly draw the curtain

The ancient winds
slide between our fingers

The crabs
bury themselves in a season
mixing forever
lichen and foam

Stars
luminous stones
adorn
your neck

The bed
is vine field
O my sun

A Leaver

I begin the moment
We aren't

Time is a corpse
are we its worms

The insect
more a power of forgetting
than all of us

He
in his quest is a meteorite
Pain is his border

The fingers of the massacre turn
one by one
fall
the heads of the hours

We are not
other
than ourselves

Neither Embers Nor Water

You make yourself one

A single ember
can she inherit
from all the fires

Triumph
which strikes me down
gospels, capitals of the setting sun
effervescent tribes

Dismembered dogma in sacks of rice
for twelve Commandments

Corpse in prayer
convalescent apocalypse

Of all suns
one alone is enough for me
to set fire to the other bank.

Also

In the dictionaries on the carpets
in the mobile phone memories
in the closed houses
in the dynasties' chests of precious stones
in the talisman of black magic
in the shell of the satyr djinn
in the black holes of the beyond
in paradise's reservoirs
filled with honey and wine
Also

In the ebony icons
on the sand of the coasts
in the towns the walkers fall from
again in the dust
in the overflowing eloquence of the telegraph wires
in the muzzled wisdom
of the charnel houses' inhabitants
Also

In the office
bones crushed between two jaws
of a barking night
at the moment when with my finger
I hide a planet
when with a hair
I slice the moon
where the pits
are bubbles which melt
Also

The clock's dial become earth
its fingers point
in all directions
the music dissects
the night's corpse.

She

In a present of torments
a rescued lake's water
She

Steps more certain of themselves
make her the shell of her pearl
She

A cloud evaporates
drop by drop
flight in brackets
a prairie's wave
flux and reflux
I mean sea
She

In her mirror
a boat
drowns itself
She

Female
drying out inkwell
feet in hell
head in paradise
She

The man she loved
falls into evening's pits
like the stone from a necklace
encircling her neck
She

sees arriving
the ideal time
to gather me
She.

Sea

My balcony
little aquarium
with its coloured fish
its algae
its old living coral

Its glass is time
its lamp the sun

For a light
that I will never see
the shell
that, each day, I break
is my hand

blue
I can't penetrate
I can't come out of again
not the one I see
but the one who sees me

Blue
which injures me
between us
surges
bellowing and foam.

Vow of the Setting Sun

I make a vow
that of the setting sun

Where are you, my cry
I saw you
in the eye of otherson the cliffs
in the sweat
never on my lips

Where are you, my wound
never have I seen you bleed
where are you, my shadow
for more than half a century
we have passed one another
in a game
between horizontal and vertical

Where are you, my tongue
don't get lost any more
come and the hands
of things and the duration
which plays with us
like rabbits

Where are you, love
what is this boat
which drifts within us
between sheets and Milky Way

Art Déco

Put a window
in the place of the chair
On the black leather armchair
leave room
for a night
which will never return

In the wardrobe
hang
the mummies of the disappeared

Let the corridor
stretch as far as the bedroom
like the arm of a siren

replace the bed
by a white cloud
the alarm clock's rung
by the bells of gothic churches
after the fall of Granada

Let the pillows
be filled with feathers of light
languishing in a rustle of silk

Let the vase
have the long neck of a camel
and be filled with cactus and thorns

Inlay
in the mirror's oval frame
a dead whale's eye
brought back from a journey
with Moby Dick

Put
in the place of the standard lamp
a black stone
planet earth
and orbit around it
praying

Replace
the curtains with peacocks
the old wall's clock by the muezzin
the Abbassid mosaic
by cubes of warm straw
from northern fields

Let the table
take the form
of human evolution's aquarium
from the discovery of the canines
to McDonald's
by way of the carnivorous tribes

Put
on library shelves
reservoirs of famine
and against clouds of grasshoppers
fans

From the ceiling
suspend paper moons
in memory of the millennial Arab people
who have become gypsies

In the bathroom
raise a cotton sky
spread on the walls
plains, prairies and seasonal rains

On the balcony
let the rope of your tresses
hang

Create a secret door
Giving onto the garden
Let it open only after death
and lead you to paradise

Earth

Earth
so high
that lying flat reaches it

Earth
which in us
has its sky

Earth
appropriating the vertical
ignoring everything horizontal

Earth
the mirror where we dig
discovering only
ourselves
burying only
ourselves

We neither approach her
nor move away
distance
is her shadow

Earth
a bubble which bursts
on time's peninsula

Maps
are passing attempts
to give her
a human face

Our capacity
to remember her
is equal to her capacity
to forget us

Flee her
penetrate her

Earth which lives
Without a place

Time which falls
its tree's pomegranate

Unite with her
in distancing
in approaching
Forgetting
is the screen
which sends her back her double

Earth
woman playing gravity
on top note, breathing the air

Earth
in us
overhanging death
while, sheep
we lick the blood of the place

Are we
her playthings
freed from all masters
or tablets of clay
fragile and fanatical

I am place
palpitating
on an earth

Al-Uzza

They called her
tree of the arid earth
wide hips
long and crumbling waist
Others called her
the giant flower of the sands
in a quiet spot
whose light is perceived
only by those who trample the desert

She
without speaking
cursed with her sisters

She
fracture
of a stolen verse

She
whose azur
is the mihrab of her femininity
and the meteor's inspiration

In woman
a path going nowhere
Did we come
from a place of no return

O idolatrous days
which, outside time
barters us with you

Dry dates
in a season
blue, white, colourless
we fall

Pause

While
the rock is beyond
shaken by the waves
the shells by the blue
a bubble
for half a century
wanders on the place's pause
the sea

While
Beirut divests itself
of its crosses and its crescents
a Phoenician skeleton
left-over of Roman sacrifices
folds itself into its navel
inscribed stones

While
temples and minarets let go
and discharge their stones
burying their odes
at the bottom of gorges of buried organs
between the neck of mount Liban
and the thighs of the Mediterranean

While
the passers-by are sol-fa
rushing down to the town's hollow
while the song is linen
tolling and drying on the vocal cords
while women are twisted bellies
in the acute angle of the look
while the mobile, on all lips
is bread of the starving
the writing
flows with ink's saliva

While
on the café table
dominating the temple's fractured columns
the cups shine
with godess's tears
final divine swag
still in our hands
No earth
other than that subdued
by migrations steps

No blood
other than the bleeding
of time
no tomb
other than the one we dug
in the inner sands
No me
other than the me
which drags me out of myself

Exercises

Figures

Monotheism
is the choice of a single god
for the universe
that also of a single colour
for blood
and of three sides
for the triangle

Forms

What does the circle like
What does it hate

Have you known
the hatred of arcs

The point
is it closed
or open

The square forms itself
from all the sides
which don't change its form

The straight line
is formed from no one
but itself

Procreation

The wound
our mother
dead after having borne us

Sentences and letters are pregnant
give birth
abort

Geography

On the expedition
in search of the unknown
the voyage is crowned
by the arrival at the spot
we never left

Awakening

The dream falls asleep
I cover it with my body
Thus, I wake up

White

White's flight
leaves you no choice

Replies multiply
white blackens

The question
which we pose tirelessly
without putting it
is white

The place
when the depths
stretch out whiteish
exists no longer

To write
is to create white

At the moment when
you breathe black

It's up to you
to seize
beneath the rays of your suns
the colours of white

To dance
child or doll
on the white rock
of sense

To dig
for the time and place
in the white
of tunnels

To seize white for yourself
to cut it
camouflage it
fake it
so it might be
on the tips of your nails
on the edges of your teeth
penetrate it
by your voice, by words
by madness and love
white then
will take hold of you
and take you to its realm

White

Clouds

What have I to do
with clouds
the probability of going
with steps which get bogged down
that of feeling
the swarming of a dry sap
which won't stop running
between red and grey

Clouds
neither lightning nor bright spell
dissipate their silent shadow
and don't wipe from them
my face

Clouds
whose chaotic dance
disguises the ends
while they drape themselves
in everything which escapes us

Clouds
following my tracks

Clouds
trying to fill the void
which kills

Clouds
bandages
drowning the haemorrhage
in the muezzin's voice

Clouds
swallowed up by rain
on the domes of heavens
on the domes of hells

Clouds
between two thumbs

Rocks

Rocks
probabilities
avowed just

Rocks
snail
scrupulous exercise, indefatigable
which takes upon itself
infinity

Pierced rocks
Howling rocks
The blood is liquid
a single drop
splits them

Rocks
mirrors of sense
where souls and bodies pile up
and shatter
human vessels

Pathway

On the water
towards me walks
without drowning
my desert

What cross
will cover your chest
When were you
my bed in the deluge

Take the wave's hand
which burns my chest

Tomorrow
my mouth will exhale
the sea's bellowing
Its rocks
in my silence
will drown their delirium
Totems and ghosts
will prostrate themselves at your feet

The beaks will laugh
The wings take off

Spume

The music
on the squares
twists the dancers' necks
The sun
in the fields
the sunflower fields

Music   Night sun
The bodies   its rays

Beirut
Turns around itself
Moon
The music
Chiaroscuro
And its hidden face

The sweat of the music
drop by drop
pours onto the sea's surface
rain
without skies
nor clouds

Haemophilic reeds
clouds
of love, of nostalgia
ages of music
dancers'
bodies

When a night
illuminates
a life's shadows
night
whose body falls dew
on the buildings' facades
the towers and terraces of cries
the sea
rears up and bellows
Where does this spume which doesn't look like me
come from

Boat

From your withering I won't make
a flower
nor from your shadow
an oar

I place a hand
on your knees
on the lunar stones
and the troubadours' rhymes

I tell the shells
the stones and the pebbles
god watching over
the remains of a planet
lost from its orbit

My half-century
stands on its ziggurat
far from Sumer
the drowning moon

Imagine

Imagine
for the ocean
a single moment of doubt
you will see it
drown itself

Imagine
for time
a single colour
you will see it
snow
melting

Imagine
for blue
a single direction
you will see it
lose
all colour

Imagine
a body
in the abyss
you will see it
sit
on your lap

Imagine
one of Allah's tears
you will see us
reeds
wasting away

Imagine
a sky
which is a bed
you will see yourself
star

Imagine
a fifth season
and you will see
a thousand and one seasons
Imagine
the sun
in a different place
in a different sky
you will see
the sea's dream

Imagine
a prison for the wind
and you will see
our houses
being cages

Imagine
the mountain
taking a single step
and you will see
the earth
leave its lair

Imagine
A shadow
Without body
And you will see
The statue of the Creation

Storm

O storm
to you my madness
I mix your ardour and your breaking loose
with the fingers of she who opens my shirt

O storm
to you my madness
I clothe myself in winter
so that migratory birds
awaken in me
and that I go to meet the destinies
predicted by palm trees

O storm
to you my madness
each night
I fall from my elevation
and abuse populations
Let them believe in
the tree-top bird
which sleeps in my pond

O storm
to you my madness
your bewilderment's clay
bleeds from my palm

O storm
to you my madness
I have neither mountains nor wings
but I have carried high
shoulders and frontiers
so you see me
among the crowds
sleeping giant

O storm
to you my madness
nothing remains between us
but this body oath
lent at birth
today
your walled refuge
and your tumble-down roof

Now

Your body
will never be a shell
your shivers
will never be waves
even if your spume
is level with my lips
Now

I share
with the salt
the taste of a sweating time
I share
with the sand's fingers
the ashes
which disperse under my eyes
the sea's fires
Now

Your lashes
brush the abyss's orbits
a moon wave
between your legs
falls drop by drop
Now

I stretch out
My sky
is a forest which catches fire
Dew
you fall
on my limbs
Now

My waking is a bed
I don't know if sleep
finds a season there
battered senseless
by thunder and lightning
Now

I dry
distances
I crush
Distances
I chew
Distances
and I read
what your knees
say
Now

Two

In the place which breathes our breath
For the tide which pulls in our moons
For the cinder which hatches in our verses
For the night which tangles our limbs
For the clay which quenches its thirst in our pits
For the shadow which takes hold of our ghosts
For the sea, for the time she is the sea
For us, for the time that we are
You are me
You and me
Two

Faces

My face
is its mirror
It isn't mine

There where she passes
Duration salivates

Her presence
Celebration
her absence
Adoration

Towards her goes the day
an old man, his stick
my body

She is a moment
conqueror
of the eternal
but remains a moment

She stops time
interrogates it
stranger
trying to find her way

She clings to the probable
no place
which gives balance to place
she points
an accusatory finger
procession
without streamers or a guide

She dreamt
of a stone
thrown without a thrower

Yesterday
she will fulfil
her history

Colosseum: Extinction Time

1

In the mausoleums, in the taverns haunted by the dream of stone, she questions Rome about the statues' tunics, the wings of the empire's chariots or the heroes' chained feet. Wave rocked by the current, she undulates in my arms.

Ropes stretched by the hands of archers posted for centuries on top of the towers of princes' palaces, we plough the streets we cross, the steps which climb us. On a patio, an execution stone slices the necks of the sun worshippers. Bunches of grapes overflowing with drunkenness, raised gardens of crowds of sunflowers.

She leans over a marble mirror. It returns the image of tresses and tender bodies. In the hollow of her breasts coils a stone which sparkles at night.

Here, we look for ourselves in the lands of declining kingdoms and we found only a pagan moon and pregnant copulas.

She, summer wind, drapes herself in a trunk, decorates herself with me, asks herself the question of the secret of the invisible sap between death and the emerald and what makes the silence in the nakedness of words. Priest of the gospels, she folds a card, loses herself amongst the ruins, the steps, the slaves of the Colosseum.

> Madam, my fingers
> at the tip of your breast
> are closer to glory
> than all History's chapters

2

Birds faint, wreaths of smoke
the tourists' gaudy shirts
Rome
kneeling ghosts
Instead of cornices
columns rise from the tombs
Entire generations bury themselves
in icons, amphorae, hills

Don't throw your stick
This present is a herd
chewing History's grass
and the magic of obscure kingdoms

On the brow
of the shepherd stone
falls a tattooed mess
The pillars of the
highest epoch crumble

3

Hello, marble
Michelangelo's lily
Raphaël's petals
The Tiber cuts Rome in two
Jesus's body cuts the earth in two

Hello, divine arm
Michelangelo's earth
I see
from the night of the eternal
stars
twinkle with the phosphorous of your bones
and the absence of sky

This planet is a prairie
The times its shepherds

What apocalypse
from the crack in a wall
foetus
a day will emerge

Notes

Page 9
H3 is the name of the region near the Iraqi/Jordanian border.

Page 10
Anu was the Sumerian sky god. Al-Mansour (714–755) was the second Caliph of the Abbassid Empire; je built Baghdad in 762.

Page 11
Al-Tawhidi (930–1023) was an Abbassid philosopher. Al-Hallaj (858–922) was a Muslim mystic. Ibn al-Muqaffa was a eighth-century Abbassid writer. Hassan ibn Hani (936–973) was court poet to the Fatimid Caliph al-Mu'izz. Al-Mutanabbi (915–965) was an Abbassid poet.

Page 12
Warka was an ancient Sumerian city.

Page 18
Inima Ilich is a Sumerian expression meaning 'when in heaven'. Al-Sawwad (the Dark Lands) is an ancient name for Iraq.

Page 23
Nassyria is a town in southern Iraq. The *toz* is a strong wind in the south of Iraq.

Page 34
Alif is the first letter of the Arab alphabet.

Page 51
Hulago Khan (1215–1265) occupied Baghdad in 1258, ending the Abbassid empire.

Page 65
Saladin defeated the Crusaders at the battle of Hattin (1187).

Page 68
Al-Taff is another name for Karbala, where Mahomet's grandson al-Hussein ibn Ali was defeated and killed in 680.
Ali ibn Abi Talib (601–661) was the fourth Caliph, and Mahomet's son-in-law.

Page 70
Utnapishtim is a character in ancient Sumerian mythology, who escapes a flood by building an ark.

Page 71
Ishtar was the Babylonian goddess of beauty and love.
Doumouzi was the Sumerian goddess of Fertility.

Page 75
The Muallaqat ('hanging poems') is a group of seven long pre-Islamic Arabic poems.

Page 76
Karradah is a Shiite area of Baghdad.

Page 83
Dhad is an emblematic letter of the Arab alphabet, used as a noun. Arabic is often called 'the language of Dhad'. *Zukat* is the Muslim practice of giving alms to the poor.

Page 86
Imru al-Qays was a great pre-Islamic poet, sometimes called the 'father of Arabic poetry'.

Page 89
Dammoun is the region of Yemen where Imru al-Qays was born. Andel and Hadramaout are places often mentioned by Imru al-Qays. The two italicised lines are from a poem by Imru al-Qays.

Page 92
For the Shiites, the Mahdi is the hidden Imam whose return they await. Nadjaf is the sacred city of the Iraqi Shiites.

Page 114
Al-Uzza was a pre-Islamic Arab goddess. The *mihrab* is the most sacred place in a Mosque.